Katherine Stinson Otero

Katherine Stinson Otero

HIGH FLYER

By Neila Skinner Petrick
Illustrated by Daggi Wallace

PELICAN PUBLISHING COMPANY
Gretna 2006

To my young readers, may your imaginations soar. —NSP

To Alexandra and Samantha, my wonderful daughters, for their support and patience. I love you. —DW

Library of Congress Cataloging-in-Publication Data

Petrick, Neila Skinner.
Katherine Stinson Otero : high flyer / by Neila Skinner Petrick ; illustrated by Daggi Wallace.
p. cm.
ISBN-13: 978-1-58980-368-8 (hardcover : alk. paper)
1. Stinson, Katherine, 1891-1977—Juvenile literature. 2. Women air pilots—United States—Biography—Juvenile literature. 3. Air pilots—United States—Juvenile literature. I. Wallace, Daggi, ill. II. Title.
TL540.O77P48 2006
629.13'092—dc22

2005024235

Printed in China

Published by Pelican Publishing Company, Inc.
1000 Burmaster Street, Gretna, Louisiana 70053

KATHERINE STINSON OTERO
HIGH FLYER

The dark-eyed girl flew through the air, her thick hair blowing in the wind. “You’re flying, Katherine!” shouted her younger sister Marjorie, who was pushing Katherine on the swing behind their house in Canton, Mississippi. The year was 1907.

“My turn next,” Marjorie called out.

The girls were still in school, and their dreams of flight were as distant as the birds soaring above them.

One day, Katherine flew in a magnificent hot-air balloon. When she landed, she told her family, " I want to learn to fly!"

"I want to learn too!" Marjorie chimed in.

Their mother, Emma Stinson, read everything she could about the inventive Wright Brothers, who had flown an airplane at Kitty Hawk, North Carolina, in 1903. She loved the idea of flying.

A few years later, Katherine and her mother visited a flying field and watched the Wright Flyers, the airplanes the Wright Brothers invented, circling above.

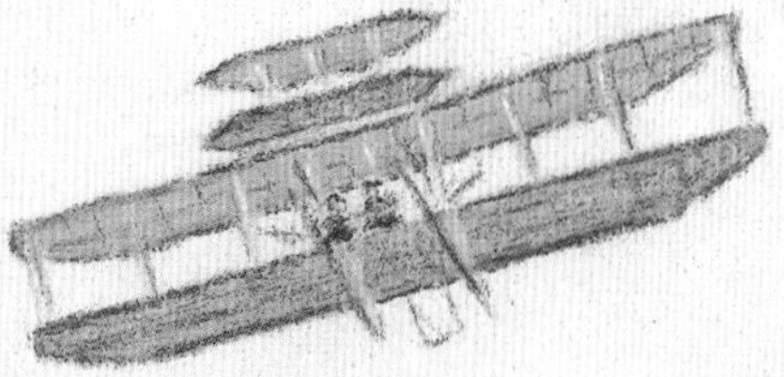

"Will they teach me to fly, Mama?"

"We'll see," said her mother.

Katherine had raised the money for flying lessons herself, selling a piano she had won in a popularity contest.

The pilots told Katherine she was too young and too small. Katherine, who weighed one hundred pounds and stood five feet tall, told them that flying relied not on strength alone but on physical and mental coordination too. They still said no. But Katherine and her mother did not give up. They spoke to many flying teachers; usually they got the same answer.

Eventually, Katherine and her mother met Max Lillie, a gentle giant who was a well-known pilot from Sweden. At first, Max told Katherine no, but she did not give up. Finally he said yes. At last, she was going to fly! Katherine was beginning the greatest adventure of her life.

The morning of July 13, 1912, dawned clear and sunny, fine weather for flying. Learning to fly was very different than it is today. The student pilot first learned to guide the airplane with simple sticks. If the student didn't fall off, he or she could learn to fly. To teach Katherine, Max set up two sawhorses with two sticks attached to two levers below. Then he moved the sawhorses, and Katherine operated the levers to control the "airplane" and keep it balanced.

Max took her flying and showed her how the airplane worked. Katherine did everything Max said. She was a good student. Finally, he announced, "You're ready to solo!"

Max repeated his instructions. "Aim the airplane into the wind and pull back. That pulls the nose up and your airplane will lift into the sky. Keep it steady," said Max. "That enables you to fly straight and level."

Max waved his cap at Katherine. "Go, Katie, go!" She began her takeoff. She could hardly believe it. She was flying alone!

She felt the airplane lifting into the sky as she pulled back on the control lever. She passed birds flying in the opposite direction and then she heard Max's voice.

"Turn to the right." She pushed on the levers and the airplane responded, turning to the right. "Now level off, Katie. Fly in a circle."

Katherine was three hundred feet in the air. Higher and higher she flew, until she was five hundred feet in the air.

"I'm flying! Look at the clouds! Look at the birds!" she shouted.

"Don't look down!" yelled Max.

"Bring it down, Katie. Push on the levers. Easy does it."
Katherine landed the plane on the grassy field, bouncing to a halt on the craft's small bicycle tires. She smiled. "I did it!"
Max said, "You're the best student I have."
That day, Katherine, nearly twenty-one years old, became only the fourth American woman licensed to fly.

Mrs. Stinson decided to open a flying school in San Antonio, Texas, near Fort Sam Houston, a U.S. Army base. Her daughter Marjorie had learned to fly soon after Katherine, and the two Stinson girls would instruct students. Their teacher, Max Lillie, joined them. Younger brothers Eddie and Jack would learn to fly as soon as they were old enough.

Katherine also flew dozens of exhibitions, first in San Antonio and then in California. A reporter in San Antonio called her "the Flying Schoolgirl" although she had graduated from high school four years earlier.

She flew the first loop-the-loop at an air show in California. She wrote *CAL* for California as well as her initials in the sky with flares and smoke. The crowds loved the young flyer.

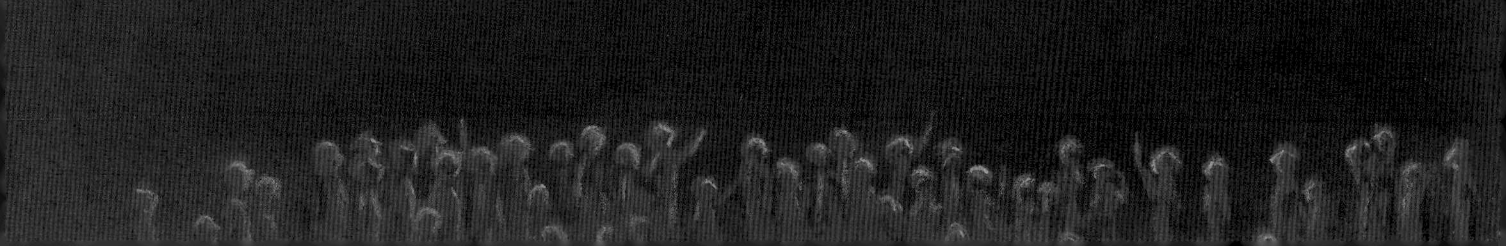

Though Katherine loved the thrill of flying, she was a very careful pilot. Katherine knew that a clean airplane was a safe airplane. Before she would take to the skies, she would spend hours checking wires and bolts and struts, making sure everything was perfect. Some pilots were not so careful.

Back home, Marjorie, who had earned the nickname "Flying Schoolmarm," was teaching young men to fly. The Great War was going on in Europe, and the airplane had become a new part of the fighting. The young Americans wanted to help. They wanted to fly.

Meanwhile, Katherine was invited to fly in Japan and China. She shipped her airplanes in huge crates on a freighter. In December 1916, she met the emperor of Japan and his wife.

She flew in front of the Imperial Palace of China and the Chinese emperor in Beijing [Peking] in March 1917. Thousands came to watch her fly.

Katherine returned to the North American continent, flying the first airmail in Canada.

She was made an honorary princess of the Manitoba tribe in Canada. Some members of her own family were of the Cherokee Nation of Native Americans.

Katherine decided to attempt to set a long-distance record flying from San Diego, California, to the Presidio in San Francisco, six hundred miles away. She would be piloting her custom-built Curtiss Speed Scout. It had an open cockpit and no instruments to tell her how much fuel she had or how high she was flying. She would fly over a mountain at Tehachapi Pass north of Los Angeles, trusting only her own vision and judgment. Before she began the flight, she carefully cleaned her airplane. She wanted to be safe.

On December 11, 1917, Katherine flew low over homes and barns, horses and cars. She forgot to bring a lunch and halfway through the journey she was hungry. Fortunately she had a canteen of water.

She knew from studying maps that the mountain lay before her. Suddenly she saw Tehachapi Pass, more than eight thousand feet high. She pulled back on the airplane's control stick. She must climb higher than she had ever flown to get across the mountain. Higher and higher she flew, pulling back on the stick as Max had taught her. She could almost touch the peak of the mountain. And then she was over the top! She leveled out her airplane and continued her journey, traveling at sixty-two miles per hour.

A few hours later, she heard strange sounds. She flew over San Francisco Bay, where small boats were tooting their horns for her. She saw the flying field at the Presidio army base. Soldiers were waiting for her with a military band.

Graceful as an eagle, she brought her plane to rest on the green grass. The large crowd erupted in cheers. She tipped her hat in their direction and then hopped out of the airplane. She had set a new distance record of 610 miles. Later, she checked her fuel tank; she had less than two gallons left.

On a visit home to San Antonio, Katherine learned that many of the flying school's students were going to war. Katherine asked the United States government for permission to fly in Europe. The answer was familiar: No.

Katherine was determined to help. She flew exhibitions throughout the United States, raising money for the Red Cross. She even raced the Empire State Express train from near Buffalo, New York, to Albany, New York, winning by half an hour.

She delivered two million dollars to the secretary of the Treasury. She asked again if she could go to Europe and fly for the U.S. Army. Again, they said no. But the Red Cross offered her a job.

Katherine drove a military ambulance taking war wounded to hospitals. The work was hard and dangerous, but Katherine did a good job. Hadn't she been the first woman in Mississippi to earn a driver's license!

While working with the wounded in Europe, Katherine became ill with tuberculosis, and soon a ship carried her back to the United States of America.

Once back in the United States, Katherine moved to New Mexico to regain her health. She had met another flyer, Miguel Otero, from Santa Fe, New Mexico, and they eventually married. He became a judge and Katherine studied architecture. She lived in New Mexico until she was eighty-six.

During her flying career, she set records, saw many lands, met a president and two emperors, and inspired thousands. Today, there are schools, an airfield, airplanes, and monuments named for Katherine Stinson Otero and the Stinson family of high flyers.